My First סידור

Book of Mitzvos

by Ruth Schild Karlinsky

photography by Isaiah Karlinsky

FELDHEIM PUBLISHERS

JERUSALEM · NEW YORK

First Published 1985
ISBN 0-87306-388-0

Copyright © 1985 by
Feldheim Publishers and Isaiah Karlinsky

FELDHEIM PUBLISHERS
POB 35002 / Jerusalem, Israel

208 Airport Executive Park
Nanuet, NY 10954

www.feldheim.com

Printed in Israel

To our children

Chana Elisheva, Yosef Dov, Tzvia Tzipora, Ephraim Menachem and Yehuda Peretz

and to all the *yeladim*

who helped us with this book!

Netilas Yadayim

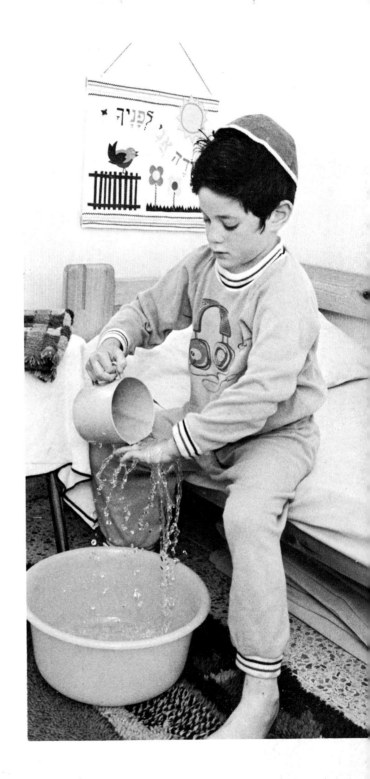

Good morning! I just woke up. I had a good rest during the night and I'm all ready to start a new day. The first thing I do every morning is say Modeh Ani — thank You Hashem for waking me up to another day. Then I wash my hands in a special way. It's called netilas yadayim. I pour water on each hand three times with our special netilas yadayim cup and I say the bracha. Now I've done the first mitzva in my day and I'm ready to do lots more. Would you like to do some too?

Tzitzis

When I was three years old, my parents gave me my first pair of tzitzis. They were new and white and just like my Abba's, only smaller. I felt so proud when I put them on. Wearing tzitzis reminds me of the 613 mitzvos in the Torah.

At night when I go to sleep, I put my tzitzis on a chair near my bed. In the morning I always remember to put them on and make the special bracha. Then I give my tzitzis a big kiss!

Tefilla

My siddur is my book of tefillos. When I daven and say the tefillos, I am talking to Hashem. We daven three times a day. Some prayers help us say thank You, Hashem. Some prayers ask Hashem to make us strong,

to take care of us, or to forgive us for something we've done.
When I open my siddur and daven, I know Hashem is listening.
During the week we usually daven in school, but sometimes I like to go
to shul with my father. I like to see the men in their white talleisim and I like
to kiss the Torah and say "amen" out loud. Sometimes I close my eyes
and add my own tefilla. Do you ever say a special prayer to Hashem too?

Brachos

Sometimes I get so hungry, I just want to grab something and eat it fast. But my Imma taught me to think first. An apple comes from a tree, but who made it grow there? When we make a bracha before we eat, we are saying that we know Hashem is the One who created this food. And by saying a bracha-acharona *after* we eat, we thank Him for having fed us.

Kibbud Rav

I like my rebbe, Reb Shmuel, so much! He is always patient and never gets angry when I make a mistake. When I came to his class at the beginning of the year, I didn't even know how to read. Now I can read very well. Reb Shmuel taught me many other things too — chumash, tefilla, dinim and mitzvos.

My teacher Morah Chaya is very special, too. Every morning when I come to school, she smiles and says, "Boker tov, Tzippy." I love to listen when she tells us about the parasha, or about a yom tov, and I try very hard to do the mitzvos we learn about.

Tzedaka

Guess what I have in my pocket? It's round and shiny and I'm saving it to put in the tzedaka box. That's right — it's a coin! The money in the tzedaka box will be given to poor people so that they can buy food and clothing for their families. I like to hear the "plink, plink" of the coins dropping into the tzedaka box, and I like the good feeling I have inside knowing that I am helping someone.

Shalom

Sometimes, when I'm with my friends, we all want to play with the same thing, like riding the same bike. We fight and shout and everyone gets angry. When that happens, I think of the word "shalom."

Shalom means peace. It's a mitzva to make
sure that you don't fight or argue with
others, and that others don't fight with you.
I think of what I can do to make peace,
because everyone's happier when there's shalom.

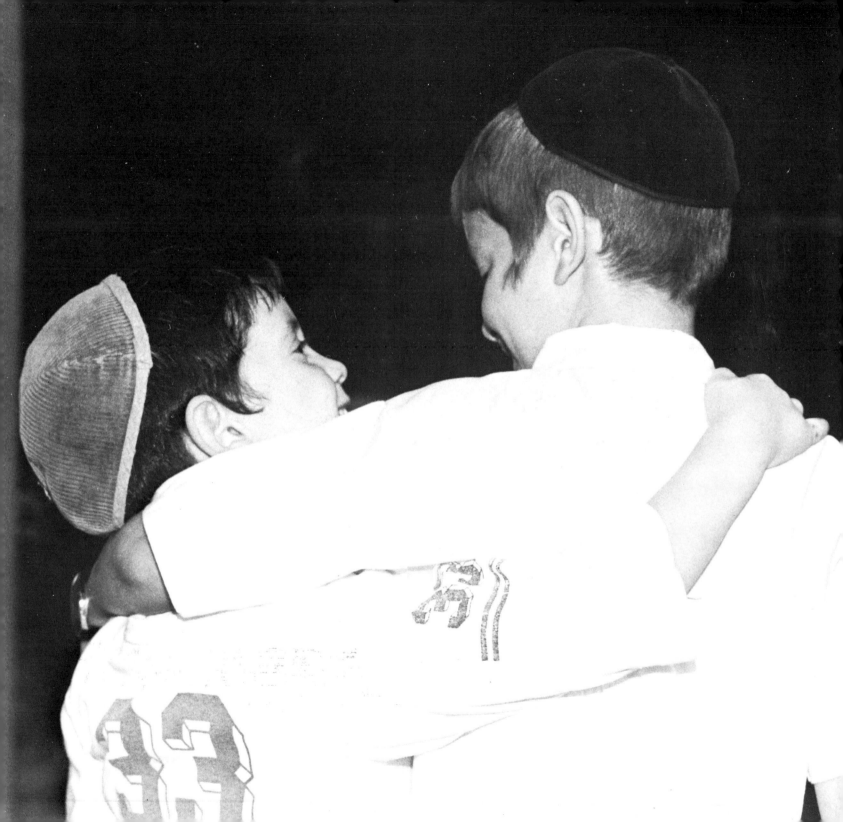

V'Ahavta L'Reyacha Kamocha

Efraim and I are very good friends. We like to be together. When he comes to my house to play, I let him choose the game he likes best. I know that if I share with him, he'll share with me. It's true, because this summer he shared his ball with me and taught me how to throw and catch. When I'm with Efraim, I feel I'm doing the mitzva of v'ahavta l'reyacha kamocha — loving my friend.

Kibbud Av Va'aym

My mother and father work very hard for me. They make sure I have good food to eat, clean clothes to wear and a nice house to live in. They help me with my homework, teach me new things, and show me how to do the mitzvos. I want to show my parents how much I love and appreciate them. That's why I try so hard to keep the mitzva of kibbud av va'aym. I pick up the toys in my room so my mother won't have to. I take my baby brother for a walk on Shabbos so my parents can rest. When Imma comes home tired, I bring her a drink. There are lots of ways to honor our parents. Can you tell how you help yours?

Sayver Panim Yafos

Today I'm drawing a picture of a face. I start with a big circle, then I make two eyes, two ears, a nose, some hair and finally a big smile. The smile turns a plain face into a happy one. When I stand in front of the mirror, I can see my own face change from plain to happy when I put on a smile.

There are so many people with whom to share a smile — my parents, my teacher, my Bubby and Zaidy, even the grocer and the schoolbus driver. It's a mitzva to greet everyone b'sayver panim yafos — in a friendly way. Doesn't it make you feel good when someone smiles at you?

Hachnasas Orchim

Someone's knocking on the door! My friends Danny and Elisheva
have come to visit. When visitors come to our house we have a chance
to do a very important mitzva called hachnasas orchim — making our
guests feel welcome. When Danny and Elisheva come inside, I take
their coats and hang them up. Then I invite them into my room to
share my toys. Later, I'll prepare a snack to eat in the kitchen.
We have a lot of fun together.

V'Hadarta Pnay Zakeyn

There's Mr. Weinstein! He's our neighbor. He always has a cheery smile and something nice to say. He's like a Zaidy for everyone on our street. When I see him coming home from the grocery store, I run to help him carry his packages, and if I meet him on the bus, I stand up to give him a seat.

It's important to treat older people with special respect. That's the mitzva of v'hadarta pnay zakeyn.

My friend Eli and I found a red cloth pencil-case on the sidewalk near our school. I wanted to walk away, but Eli reminded me of the mitzva of hashavas aveyda — returning lost objects to their owners. There was a clue inside the pencil case — "Yanky Cohen" was written in gold letters on one of the pencils. We knew a Yanky Cohen, so we ran as fast as we could to ask if the pencil-case was his. It was, and Yanky was very glad to have his pencil-case again.

Hashavas Aveyda

Hasaras Michshol

Hasaras michshol means removing anything which might hurt someone. That's why I get so angry when I see something like this bicycle right in the doorway. Besides making the house look messy, bikes in the wrong place are dangerous. Someone could trip and fall and really get hurt. When you're finished riding, your bike has to be put away. Puzzles, jumpropes, or building blocks shouldn't be left in the middle of the floor either. Do you have a good, safe place for the toys in your house?

Tza'ar Ba'aley Chayim

Our teacher took us to a zoo, and we all had a chance to pet and feed the animals. We were very careful to be gentle because we learned about the special mitzva of tza'ar ba'aley chayim. That means we must never tease or hurt a living creature. We should be kind to all animals and take good care of our pets.

Can you see how gently the girl in the picture is petting the donkey?

Meat / Milk

Before I set the table for supper, I ask my mother an important question. "Will we be eating milchig — dairy — or fleishig — meat? If it's meat, we'll need the red checked tablecloth, the green flowered dishes, and the fleishig silverware. If it's a dairy meal, I'll have to get the

blue tablecloth, the dishes with the gold stripe, and the milchig
silverware. Even the dish towels we use are different. In a Jewish
house, milk and meat don't mix!
Do you know the difference between milchig and fleishig in your house?

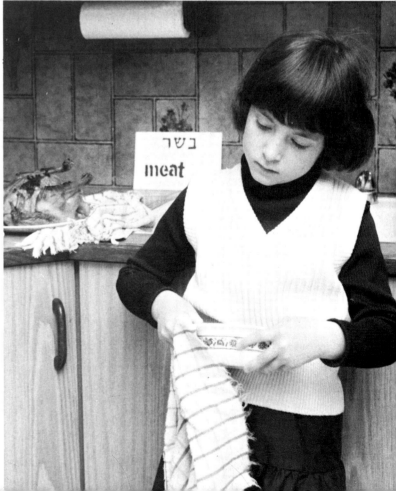

Talmud Torah

This year in school we finished learning aleph-beis and started learning chumash. Our Rebbe told us that learning Torah is a big mitzva, and the more we learn the smarter we get. I like to sit on my father's lap and show him what I've learned with my rebbe. On Shabbos, my older sister reviews what she learned in school all week. If she doesn't understand something, she asks my father or mother and they always explain.

Kriyas Shma

I had a very busy day doing mitzvos, and now it feels good to be in my nice, soft bed. I want to tell Hashem how much I love Him so I put my hand over my eyes and say Shma Yisrael, word by word, very slowly. I'm never afraid at night, not of the dark or anything else. Hashem sends special angels to watch over us while we're sleeping — one on each side of my bed.

I know I'm tired because I can feel my eyes starting to close . . . good night . . . layla tov. . . . .

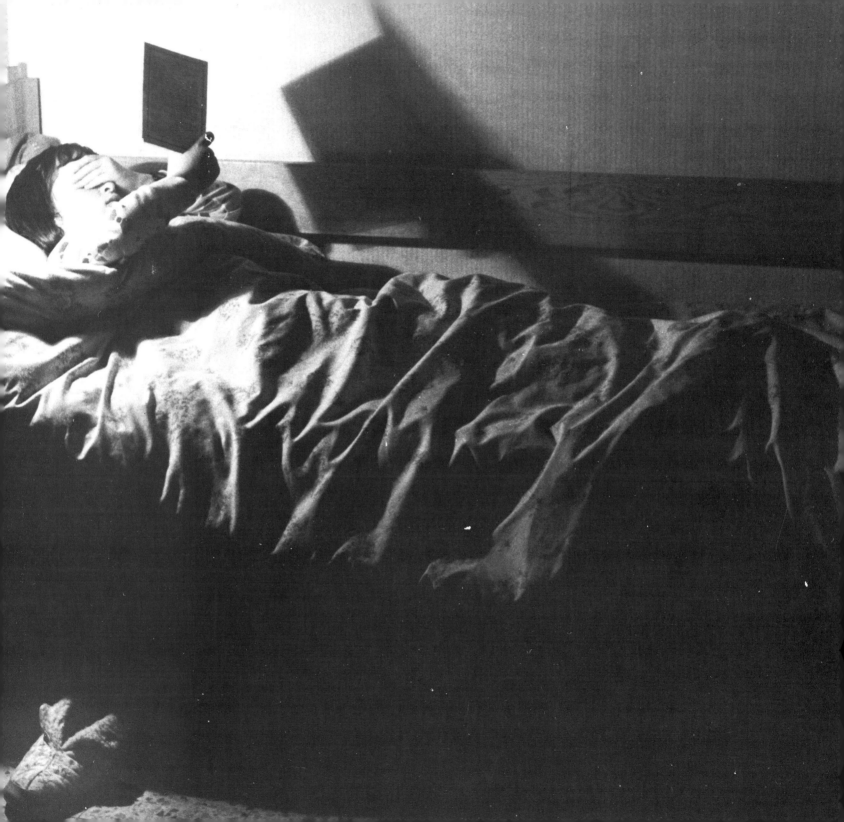

ACKNOWLEDGMENT

The idea for this book, including sample text and photographs, was originally submitted to Feldheim Publishers by Ruth Lipson.

Mrs. Lipson wishes to extend her warm thanks and appreciation to the following people who helped her prepare the proposal and the initial draft. To Menachem and Leah Adelman and to all the children and their parents who agreed to be photographed; to Mr. and Mrs. Irwin Benjamin, and to Rabbi and Mrs. Louis El'Chonen who helped underwrite the cost of the original photography; to her Aunt Jean and Uncle Paul who wished to express their love and dedication; to Dr. and Mrs. Henry Rhein; to Dr. and Mrs. Leonard Sacharow whose contribution was given in gratitude to the Jewish Center for Special Education; to Mr. and Mrs. Harold Shapero who donated to the project in honor of their great-grandson Lyisch; and to many more individuals who prefer to remain anonymous.